This edition published by Parragon Ltd in 2014 and distributed by

Parragon Inc.
440 Park Avenue South, 13th Floor
New York, NY 10016
www.parragon.com

ISBN 978-1-4723-5227-9

Printed in China

Contents

About this book 4

Tools & Techniques 5

Sewing kit 6
Fabrics 8
Stuffing 10
Some stitches 12
Start to stitch 14
How to appliquè 16

Things to Make

Cozy egg covers 18
Pom-pom fun 20
Headband 22
Using denim 24
Motif T-shirt 26
Square cushion cover 28
Long alien cushion 30
Tiny toadstool pincushion 32
Arm warmers 34
Shopping bag 36
Clutch a clutch 38
Button bracelet 40
Build a blanket 42
Patchwork Charlie Chick 44
Felt teddy bear 46
Felt dolly 50
Mini mascots 52
Sock monster 54
Sock rabbit 56
Fabric flower brooch 58
Sparkly rock chick button 60
Sweet dreams eye mask 62
Credits 64

About this book

Are you GIRLIE? A ROCK CHICK? Into QUIRKY AND TOTALLY INDIVIDUAL STYLE?

Take the projects in this book and let your imagination run wild.

There are NO limits.

The crafts and instructions are specific enough to help out a beginner, but they've got enough variety to please the pickiest of pros. Whatever your level, this book gives you the skills and guidance you need to make your own things.

The best part about the projects is that they're totally eco-friendly and low cost. All you have to do is reduce, reuse, and recycle—and raid your wardrobe! Use clothes you've grown out of, stray buttons, ratty blankets, even old curtains ...

JUST DON'T FORGET TO ASK YOUR PARENTS FIRST!

HELLO

TOOLS & TECHNIQUES

5

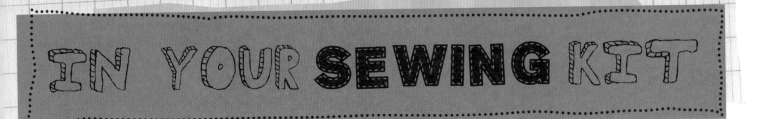

IN YOUR SEWING KIT

You really don't need too many materials to get started. This book comes with some of them, and the rest you can find at fabric stores or even around your house. If you need a bag to keep everything in, why not make it yourself? Check out the next section!

Every sewing kit should have:

Needles

A mixture of needles is best: use medium-length, sharp needles for general sewing and shorter quilting needles for the really finicky work. Needles with long eyes are for embroidery.

Eye

Sewing thread

A whole load of different colors is a must for the modern sewer. You normally want to match the color of the thread to the fabric, but sometimes you want it to stand out, so pick boring colors, such as black and white, and bold colors, such as purple, too!

Embroidery thread

Embroidery thread is much thicker than sewing thread and is used to decorate rather than attach fabric together.

6

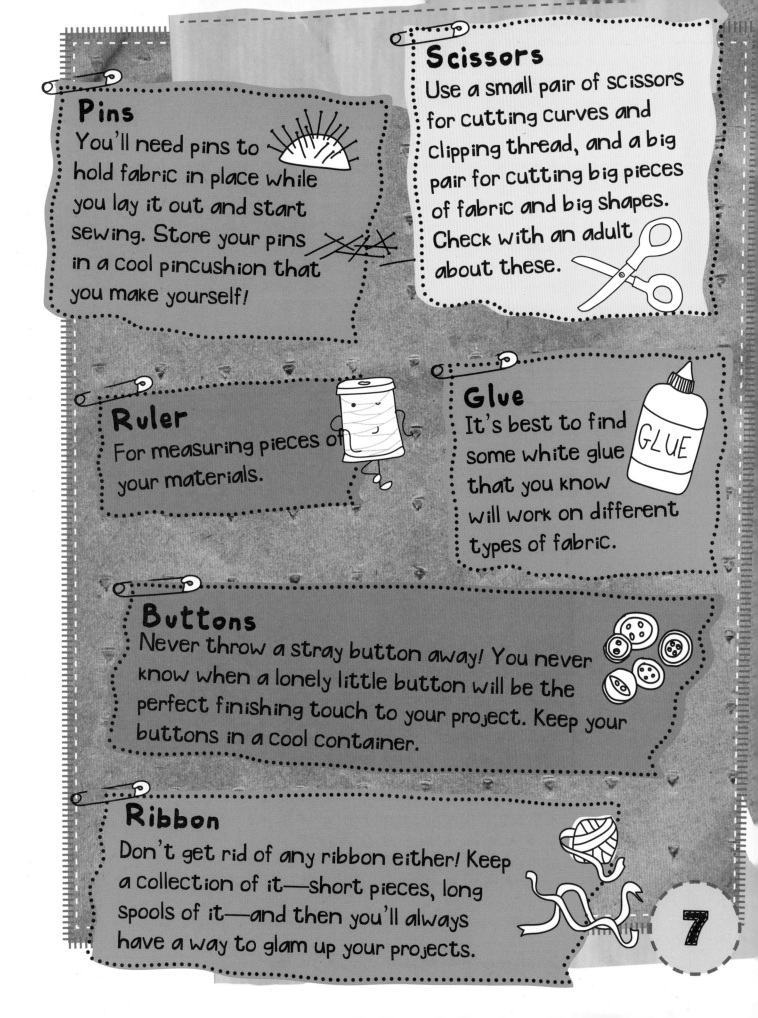

Pins

You'll need pins to hold fabric in place while you lay it out and start sewing. Store your pins in a cool pincushion that you make yourself!

Scissors

Use a small pair of scissors for cutting curves and clipping thread, and a big pair for cutting big pieces of fabric and big shapes. Check with an adult about these.

Ruler

For measuring pieces of your materials.

Glue

It's best to find some white glue that you know will work on different types of fabric.

GLUE

Buttons

Never throw a stray button away! You never know when a lonely little button will be the perfect finishing touch to your project. Keep your buttons in a cool container.

Ribbon

Don't get rid of any ribbon either! Keep a collection of it—short pieces, long spools of it—and then you'll always have a way to glam up your projects.

FABRICS

When you're sewing, remember that every fabric is different.

FELT

Felt is the easiest material to handle. Even if you're just starting out, you (yes, you!) can handle it. Felt is easy to cut and doesn't fray. Remember that felt doesn't like to be bathed and might act up if you try to put it in water!

COTTON

If you're going to use cotton (such as an old shirt), if it hasn't already shrunk, wash it. That way, it won't shrink if you wash it after you make it into something new, and your new item will smell nice and fresh (and not like an old shirt)!

FLEECE

An old fleece is a great material for making a new scarf, but just remember that fleece is a little stretchier than cotton and felt, so be careful not to pull on it when you're cutting and sewing.

LEATHER

If you're lucky enough to be allowed to use an old, thin piece of soft leather, be extra careful and maybe even use a thimble while you're sewing. Leather is really thick, and needles don't like to go through it very easily.

You'll need to stuff most of these super-cute projects to add the cuddly and squishable factor. There are loads of options for different stuffing materials you can use.

Try these ideas:

Cotton or polyester filling

This is the traditional stuffing, and it can be bought at a range of stores. If you get a high-quality filler, you'll get a professional-looking project. No lumps or anything!

Dried beans

This is another popular choice that creates a different feel. This is good for juggling balls, door stops, and projects where you want a beanie feel.

Dried rice

Here's another popular option, similar to dried beans. And you probably already have some at home! Just ask your parents if you can use it first.

Potpourri

See if you can track down some scented filling such as dried lavender. A softie stuffed with a scented filling makes an awesome gift!

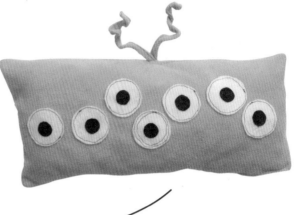

You can even try socks, yarn, tissues, or newspaper if you want to use what you've got lying around at home. This won't feel as professional as cotton filling, but it will make each softie unique!

When you sew up the hole you've used to stuff your softie, try this trick to make the hole invisible:

Fold the fabric inside, tuck it in neatly, and use tiny stitches to close the hole. The rough edges will be secretly hidden!

11

SOME stitches

Running stitch

The running stitch is the most basic of stitches. You simply bring your needle up through your fabric at point A and down again at point B to make a little line of thread. If you keep doing this in a straight line, going in and out of the fabric, you can sew a basic seam and stitch fabric together.

Backstitch

Backstitching is taking the running stitch to the next level. Start at point B, bringing your needle up through the fabric, and stitch back down through point A. Then bring your needle under the fabric, past point B, come up at point C, and then down again at point D. Because you're going over the stitches, this is a supersolid way to stitch two pieces of fabric together.

12

Satin stitch

Use the running stitch, but do a whole bunch side by side to make a shiny, satiny row of stitches.

B → A

Split running stitch

This is just like the running stitch except that instead of bringing your needle up beside each stitch, you bring it up in the middle of the previous stitch, splitting it. You'll end up with a row of overlapping stitches. Because the stitches are so tight together, this type of stitch is good for curves and lettering.

B A
D C

STARTING the STITCHES

You're probably thinking all this sounds so awesome and I can't wait to get started ... but how DO I start?

- First, get your needle and thread ready.
- Cut a piece of thread about an arm's length.
- Then thread your needle (get the thin little piece of thread through the tiny hole in the needle).

Have patience! You can do it!

- Once the thread is through the hole, move the needle to the middle of the thread and fold the thread in half. Having a double layer of thread will keep your stitches superstrong.
- Finally, tie the two ends together with a knot near the end of the thread. You may need to tie a few knots on top of each other, so the thread doesn't slip through your fabric.

Finishing the stitches

OK, so you know how to get started, but once you start, how do you stop? You can't just leave your needle hanging there! To finish up, do a few stitches on top of each other to secure the thread, or, if you want the end to look supertidy, sew through the thread on the underside of the fabric a few times— no one will know the extra stitches are there but you.

When you're happy that your stitches aren't going anywhere, snip the thread close to the fabric—but not so close that it comes right out! Then your needle is finally free.

Wait, there's one more thing!

Sewing on a button!

1. Thread your needle with some thread that matches the color of the button.

2. Lay the button in place on the material.

3. From under the material, push the needle through the fabric and up through one of the holes of the button.

4. Pull the thread all the way up, until the knot is tight against the fabric.

5. Next—you can probably guess—is to go back down through another hole in the button, and straight down through the fabric.

6. Repeat this three more times to secure the button in place. If the button has four holes, do this three times diagonally one way and three times diagonally in the other two holes.

7. When you've finished, make sure your needle is under the fabric. Thread it through the thread under the material and tie a double knot.

And that's it!

HOW TO APPLIQUÉ

What does appliqué mean, anyway? It's simple, really. We're cutting out shapes of one fabric and sticking them to another. This T-shirt is done this way.

We're going to use fusible webbing to do the sticking.

I was done with appliqué!

Your final picture is going to be a mirror image of the template you use. It gets flipped over, so if you're doing letters, remember to draw them backward!

How to appliqué

1. Trace a pattern from a template at the back of the book, photocopy one of the templates, or draw your own onto the paper side of the fusible webbing.

2. Cut roughly around the edges of the shape. This is your chance to be messy. It doesn't have to be perfect yet!

3. Place the shape adhesive side down on the fabric you're using for the shape. Ask an adult to iron it in place. If you're using patterned material, make sure you attach the paper to the non-patterned side.

4. No more Mr. Messy Guy! Cut carefully around the edges of your shape. This time you're cutting the paper and the fabric because they are stuck together.

Fabric

Template

5. Peel the backing paper off the shape and turn it over. The side with the adhesive on it will be rough, and the other side will be untouched, so you'll know which is which if you get confused.

6. Place the shape on the side of a bag, the front of a pair of jeans, or the back of a T-shirt. Ask an adult to iron it in place with a cool iron. Press the iron down instead of sliding it on the material, so the shape doesn't move around.

7. Lift the iron and check out your awesome appliqué. Ta-da! That shape should be stuck on good!

COZY EGG COVERS

Keep your boiled eggs cozy with these super-cute egg warmers.

To make the penguin, YOU'LL NEED:

- 2 pieces of black felt, about 4 inches at the base
- 2 white felt circles
- 1 small triangle of orange felt for the beak
- 2 buttons
- Patterned fabric for his belly, about 3 inches at the base
- 2 pieces of black felt for the wings
- White and black sewing thread and white glue

HERE'S WHAT YOU DO:

1. Sew or glue the white felt circles to a piece of black felt, and sew the buttons on.

2. Glue on the beak.

3. Glue or sew on the patterned belly fabric.

4. Place the penguin face down on the other piece of black felt.

Base layer

Top layer

Wings in between

5. Place the wings between the fabric. Sew around the penguin sides and top, but don't touch the bottom.

6. Turn right side out.

Use the same process to make an edgy egg warmer. Try a patch and patterned fabric instead of felt and cute penguin features.

POM-POM FUN

Pom-poms are adorable little pals.

HERE'S WHAT YOU DO:

1. Use a compass to draw a circle about 2 inches across on the cardboard and cut out. From the center of the circle, draw another smaller circle, 1 inch across, and cut this out. Repeat to make one more ring.

2. Put the two pieces of cardboard together to get one sturdy donut.

3. Wind the yarn around the donut. Work your way around until all the cardboard is well covered.

4. Ask an adult to help you cut all the way around the outer edge of the donut, snipping the yarn as you go.

5. Slide a piece of yarn between the two pieces of cardboard and wrap it around the donut. Pull tight to tie all the pieces of yarn together. Then remove the cardboard.

6. Fluff up the pom-pom, and trim it to make it nice and neat. Glue on the eyes and ribbon!

HEADBAND

Floppy, annoying bangs will be a thing of the past with this project! Even if you don't have bangs to hold back, a headband can be a cool accessory for any style!

YOU'LL NEED:

❀ 2 pieces of patterned or plain fabric, about 16 x 2.5 inches

❀ A piece of elastic, 6 inches long

HERE'S WHAT YOU DO:

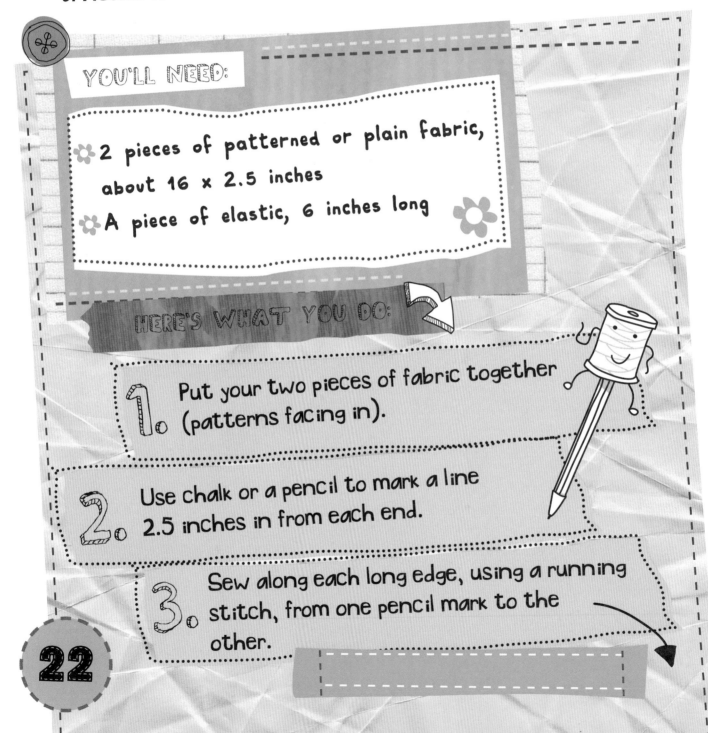

1. Put your two pieces of fabric together (patterns facing in).

2. Use chalk or a pencil to mark a line 2.5 inches in from each end.

3. Sew along each long edge, using a running stitch, from one pencil mark to the other.

4. Turn right side out.

5. Slide your elastic inside one of the open ends. Push it up to your pencil mark and pin in place.

← Elastic

6. Repeat step 5 with the other end of the elastic and the other headband opening.

7. Secure the elastic at each end by doing backstitch across each line.

USING DENIM

Do you have jeans with holes in the knees or that are too short for you now? Don't throw them out! You can get a whole new wardrobe item out of them!

ALERT! ALERT! Ask an adult to help when you're cutting and sewing denim.

MAKE DENIM SHORTS OR A SKIRT

Turn your jeans into shorts or a skirt and no one will ever know they nearly went in the trash. You can do this with other pants too.

HERE'S WHAT YOU DO:

1. Ask an adult to iron the jeans so you're working with a like-new piece of fabric.

2. Fold the legs on top of each other, along the fly.

3. Mark where you want the shorts or skirt to end, adding an extra inch for the hem. Use a ruler to draw a straight line from seam to seam on each leg. Make sure this line is under the pockets and crotch.

4. Cut along each line. You'll now have a pair of shorts! All you need to do now is turn the bottom edges of the legs inward about an inch and use a nice thick needle to sew the hem.

5. To make a skirt, you need to use a needle or scissors to take out the stitches that make the crotch. Do this a few stitches at a time. Ask an adult to help you.

6. Pin the left and right front pieces of the denim (the pieces that used to be the crotch) one over the other, then sew them together. Do the same for the back pieces.

7. Turn the bottom of the skirt up an inch toward the inside. Ask an adult to press it down, and then sew around it to make a nice, clean hem.

transformation

MOTIF T-SHIRT

Just hanging out for a while ...

To make this supercute T-shirt, you'll need:

- Brown felt fabric cut to the shape of a bear (use the template at the back of this book)
- White felt fabric cut to the shape of a bear, but bigger than the brown felt version
- White fabric for the eyes and mouth
- Pink felt for the inner ears
- Embroidery thread
- Black sewing thread

HERE'S WHAT YOU DO:

1. Doing a running stitch with your embroidery thread, sew the brown and white felt bear pieces together.

2. Glue the pink parts to complete the inner ears.

Running stitch

3. In the center of each white piece of eye felt, do a few small running stitches very close together with the black sewing thread.

Satin stitch

4. On the white piece of mouth felt, use a satin stitch to sew on the nose and mouth with the black cotton thread.

TIP: Use a pencil to draw a faint line for the nose and mouth before stitching.

5. Glue the eye and mouth pieces of felt to the brown bear face.

6. Glue or appliqué the face to the front of your T-shirt.

LET IT DRY! THEN WEAR THAT BEAR!

SQUARE CUSHION COVER

This cushion is simple, yet it makes a serious splash on your couch. First, find a plain cushion that needs a cover.

Tweet

YOU'LL NEED:

- 1 square piece of plain fabric, about 1 inch longer on each side than your cushion
- 1 square piece of patterned fabric, the same size as the plain fabric square
- Fabric, buttons, felt, ribbons—anything to make your cushion stand out!
- Velcro, the length of one side of the plain fabric square
- Black and white sewing thread, white glue

HERE'S WHAT YOU DO:

1. Sew, glue, or appliqué your design onto the plain fabric square.

GLUE

2. Turn the design face down and sew the Velcro piece along the bottom of the square.

Velcro strip

28

3. Turn the patterned fabric face down and sew the other part of the Velcro along one edge.

4. Place the design face down against the patterned fabric square (pattern facing the design).

Make sure the Velcro pieces are lined up!

5. Sew along the two sides and the top of the cushion using the backstitch, leaving the Velcro edges open.

6. Turn the cover right side out. Then put the cushion in and keep it secure by sticking the Velcro together.

LONG ALIEN CUSHION

This extraterrestrial cushion will bring extraordinary attention to your couch or bed!

YOU'LL NEED:

- 2 pieces of fabric, about 24 x 12 inches. Fleece works well!
- 7 white felt circles, for the eyes
- 7 small black felt circles, for the pupils
- 2 pieces of fabric or felt, 6 x 1.5 inches, for the antennae
- 2 pieces of thin wire, each 6 inches long
- White and black sewing thread
- Stuffing and white glue

TO MAKE THE EYES:

For a cool alien effect, do a running stitch around each white circle with black thread, and then glue the black pupil to the middle of each eye.

TO MAKE THE ANTENNAE:

Fold one thin piece of fabric in half with the wire inside, and sew all the way around using a running stitch. Do the same for the other antenna.

Folded in half

Wire inside

TO MAKE THE CUSHION:

Put the two pieces of fabric together (outsides facing in), and sew around the outside using the backstitch, leaving a small gap. Turn right side out and stuff, then sew up the small hole using the split running stitch.

Glue all seven eyes on. Sew the bottom of each antenna to the top of the cushion's back and then twist them for the finishing touch.

Hey human, I'm watching you!

TINY TOADSTOOL PINCUSHION

Have you ever seen such an adorable place to keep your pins? Super cute!

YOU'LL NEED:

White felt, 1 x 6 inches

1 circle of cardboard, 2 inches across

1 circle of red felt, 3.5 inches across

Small round circles of white felt

Black thread, stuffing, white glue

HERE'S WHAT YOU DO:

 Starting at a short edge, roll the white felt into a cylinder. Draw on the eyes and mouth.

 Unroll the felt and sew the face on with black thread.

 Now roll the felt up again and glue the end in place.

Place the red felt flat on a table. Put a little stuffing in the middle and then place the cardboard on top.

Cardboard
Stuffing
Red felt

 Do a loose running stitch around the edge of the red felt circle, pulling as you work so the middle gap is being closed over the stuffing and cardboard.

 When you're done, there should be a small hole under the cap of the toadstool. Wedge the white roll just inside this and glue in place.

Glue the white circles to the top of the toadstool.

Leave to dry, then start pinning!

33

ARM WARMERS

Are your arms always getting cold? Then they need some arm warmers to warm them up! And if you're not a cold-armed person ... well, arm warmers make an awesome fashion statement, too.

YOU'LL NEED:

An old pair of long socks (wash them first!)

Sewing thread

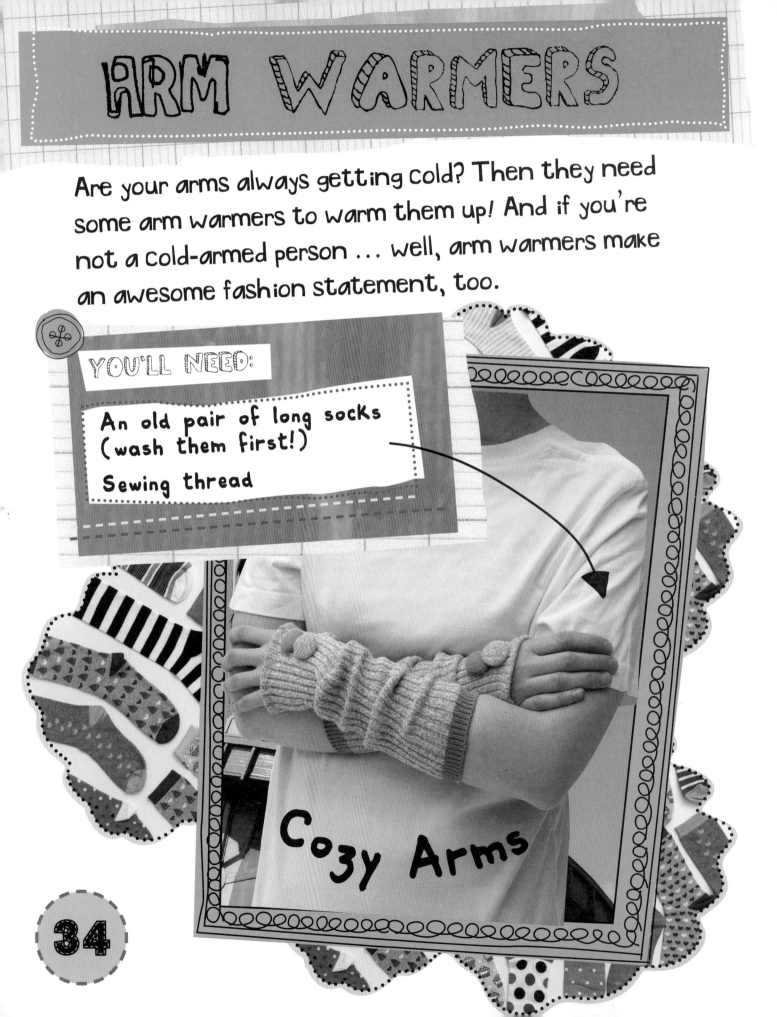

Cozy Arms

HERE'S WHAT YOU DO:

1. Put your hands inside each sock and pull them right up to your elbows. Use a pen to draw a faint diagonal line where your thumb starts and another line across your knuckles (on the sock, not on your hand!).

2. Take your hands out and cut along the lines you've drawn.

3. Turn the socks inside out.

4. Fold the seams of each hole you've cut down about 1/2 inch and sew around the holes using a running stitch. You'll do a full circle to sew the fold down. But be careful! Make sure you don't sew up the hole by accident.

5. Turn the socks the right way out again.

TIP:
Try covering buttons with the scrap pieces of sock and sew these onto your new arm warmers.

35

SHOPPING BAG

YOU'LL NEED:

- Scissors
- Needle & thread
- 1 large piece of strong, plain fabric, 16 X 22 inches
- 1 smaller piece of patterned fabric, 8 x 14 inches

HERE'S WHAT YOU DO:

1. Cut the plain fabric to measure 16 x 22 inches.

16 inches

22 inches

2. Cut the patterned fabric to 11 x 14 inches and sew on top of the plain fabric with an equal gap at all sides.

11 x 14 inches

16 inches

22 inches

3. Then fold the fabric in half along the long side, and stitch along the side and bottom.

Fold here

Warning! Don't sew up the top of your bag! Just sew along the white dotted line.

Use running stitches: quick & easy!

4. Cut two thin strips of the plain fabric to measure 1 x 16 inches.

1 inch

16 inches

Fold here

Sew here

5. Fold the strips in half lengthwise. Sew all the way along the edges.

6. Make the strips into handles. Sew one end inside the front panel of the bag, 1.5 inches from the left edge. Then curl the strip around and sew the other end 1.5 inches from the right edge. Repeat this on the back panel of the bag with the other strip.

OUT

and

ABOUT

7. Adorn your bag with **LOVELINESS!** Try your fave pattern, such as a skull and crossbones motif! **AHOY, ME HEARTY!**

with my **NEW BAG!**

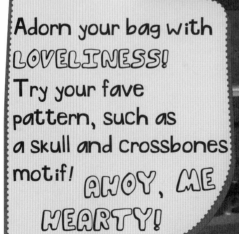

CLUTCH A CLUTCH!

YOU'LL NEED:

◎ Patterned fabric for the outside, roughly 23 x 9 inches

◎ Bright piece of felt for the lining, also roughly 23 x 9 inches

◎ Small pieces of fabric, buttons, or patches to decorate

◎ A fastener and a needle

◎ Colorful thread to complement the pattern of fabric you've chosen

Tweet
Tweet

HERE'S WHAT YOU DO:

1. Cut the fabric and felt into a 23 x 9-inch rectangle and lay the felt on top of the fabric.

23 inches
9 inches
Felt
Fabric

2. Use a straight running stitch to sew the felt and fabric together. Go all the way around the rectangle.

3. Fold the bottom of the rectangle up about 6 inches, making sure that the patterned fabric faces out and the felt is on the inside.

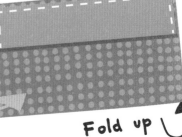

Fold up

4. Fold the top part of the rectangle down to make the flap of the clutch bag, and pin it carefully in place.

Fold down

5. Now—this is the fun part—cut the fabric in any shape you like, grab buttons or patches, and start decorating! Place the pieces onto the clutch without attaching them.

HELLO

TIP:
You can stitch letters onto your clutch using a split running stitch.

6. Once you're happy with your design, stick the pieces down with glue or, if you're super adventurous, try appliqué (see page 18).

Running stitch

7. Use a running stitch to stitch the bag together—but only go up to the flap on each side.

HELLO

8. Finally, stick your fastener to the inside of the bag, roughly in the middle, to keep your little clutch bag shut while you're out and about.
Now you're ready to SHOW IT OFF!

Hello

BUTTON BRACELET

For this project, you'll need loads and loads of buttons and a long piece of stretchy beading cord that's thin enough to fit through the button holes.

Thread the cord through the button holes, pushing each button as far as you can to the end of the bracelet, until you have a piece of cord filled with buttons long enough to fit around your wrist.

Tie a knot tight against the last button to hold all the buttons securely in place.

Tie the two ends together.

Put the bracelet on your wrist!

BUILD A BLANKET

THERE ARE LOADS OF DIFFERENT WAYS TO MAKE A QUILT OR BLANKET.

Try piecing more pieces of fabric together for a real patchwork look for your quilt ...

Or go with different PATTERNS and SHAPES to change the style.

42

Instead of a decorative quilt, try a snuggly blanket made of fleece. If you don't have an old fleece shirt as big as a blanket, you can buy a yard of fleece at a fabric store for a low price. Fabric stores usually have plenty of different patterns to choose from, too.

When you've got your fleece, sew shapes to it, or simply snip into one end, making 2-inch cuts in every 1/2 inch to create a fringed effect.

If you want a gift that leaves a lasting impression, a fleece like this is the way to go. It's simple and inexpensive, but such a thoughtful present.

PATCHWORK CHARLIE CHICK

This is another little guy who can stay small or be blown up nice and big. Go crazy with the template!

YOU'LL NEED:

- 2 pieces of white felt, cut to a chick shape
- 1 piece of red felt, cut to the shape of hair
- 2 pieces of red felt, cut to the shape of feet
- 1 piece of orange felt, cut to the shape of a beak
- Patterned fabric, about 2 x 4 inches
- Stuffing
- Black and white sewing thread

HERE'S WHAT YOU DO:

1. Sew eyes to one piece of the white felt using the black thread and a split stitch.

2. Sew or glue the beak to the face.

3. Sew the patterned fabric to the bottom half of the chick body front using the running stitch.

4. Place the chick face down on top of the second piece of felt chick body.

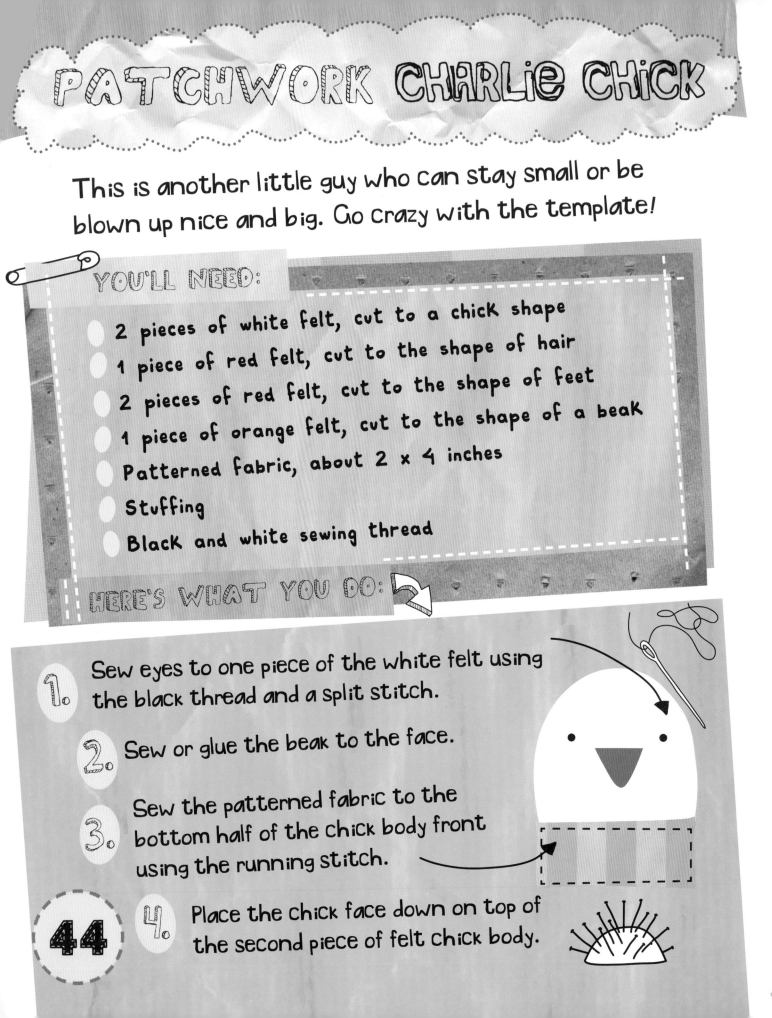

5. Put the feet and hair in place between the two pieces of fabric.

Chick face down

2nd piece of chick felt body

6. Sew all the way around, securing the feet and hair as you work and leaving a small hole at the side of the chick.

7. Turn the chick the right way out.

8. Stuff your chicklet with stuffing and sew up the hole.

And there you have Charlie!

FELT TEDDY BEAR

This character is a bit more complicated to make, so let's break it down.

Use the templates at the back of this book to get the right bear shape!

To make the HEAD AND EARS, YOU'LL NEED:

- 2 circles of white felt for eyes
- 1 piece of white felt for the mouth
- 2 large pieces of brown felt, cut to the shape of a teddy bear head
- 2 pieces of patterned fabric, cut to the shape of ears
- 2 pieces of brown felt, cut to the shape of ears
- Black sewing thread
- Stuffing and white glue

MAKE THE EARS FIRST:

1. Place one piece of the patterned ear fabric and one piece of the brown ear felt back to back (pattern facing in).

2. Sew all the way around the ear, leaving a small hole at the bottom.

3. Use the little hole to turn the ear right side out.

4. Pinch the bottom of the ear, bringing the two bottom corners toward each other, folding in on the patterned side.

5. Sew the bottom together to create a pinched ear.

6. Repeat steps 1 to 5 with the other ear-shaped fabric and felt, so you don't have a one-eared teddy bear!

NOW MAKE TEDDY'S HEAD:

1. To give your teddy bear pupils, use your black thread to sew several times in the middle of the white felt circles.

2. Stitch a nose onto the mouth-shaped felt.

GLUE

3. Sew or glue the eyes and mouth to one piece of brown head-shaped felt.

4. Lay the plain head piece of felt down. Position the ears on this piece, fabric side down. Then place the face piece of felt face down against the plain felt. Your ears should be between the pieces of felt.

5. Sew around the face, attaching the front and back and making sure the ears are secured as you go. Leave a small hole at the bottom.

47

Continues on next page

FELT DOLLY

To make a little dolly, use the exact same steps as for the teddy bear on pages 34 to 37, but use different colors of felt and different facial features to make this softie girlie rather than furry! Add stuffed arms and legs, too!

Attach the hair and clothes after you've put your doll together.

GIRLS JUST WANNA HAVE FUN!

51

MINI MASCOTS

Use the techniques on the previous pages to make yourself a tiny softie. Make him out of felt or socks or whatever material you like best—the only difference from the earlier projects is that he's mini!

Very small but very CUTE

Be creative—go cute, quirky, or COOL!

Take your mini mascot with you everywhere for good luck and for fun!

He likes to hang off tote bags ...

and hang out in the park ...

be careful he doesn't get lost out there!

Use one of the templates at the back of this book, or draw your own character to cut out.

SOCK MONSTER

To make this scary (but still super-cute) monster, **YOU'LL NEED:**

- 1 old sock (washed, please!)
- 1 small piece of felt, cut to the shape of a tooth
- 1 large button
- 1 covered button (wrap material around the button and fasten with glue or stitches at the back)
- Black ribbon, about 5 inches long
- Black sewing thread
- Stuffing and white glue

HERE'S WHAT YOU DO:

1. Cut your sock across at the heel, so you're only working with the flat foot part.

2. To give your monster eyes, sew the two buttons to the sock.

3. To give your monster a mouth, use the running stitch to attach the ribbon to the sock.

4. Glue on the tooth.

5. Fill your monster with the stuffing, making him as chubby or skinny as you like.

6. Sew up the opening of the sock so none of the monster's insides come oozing out.

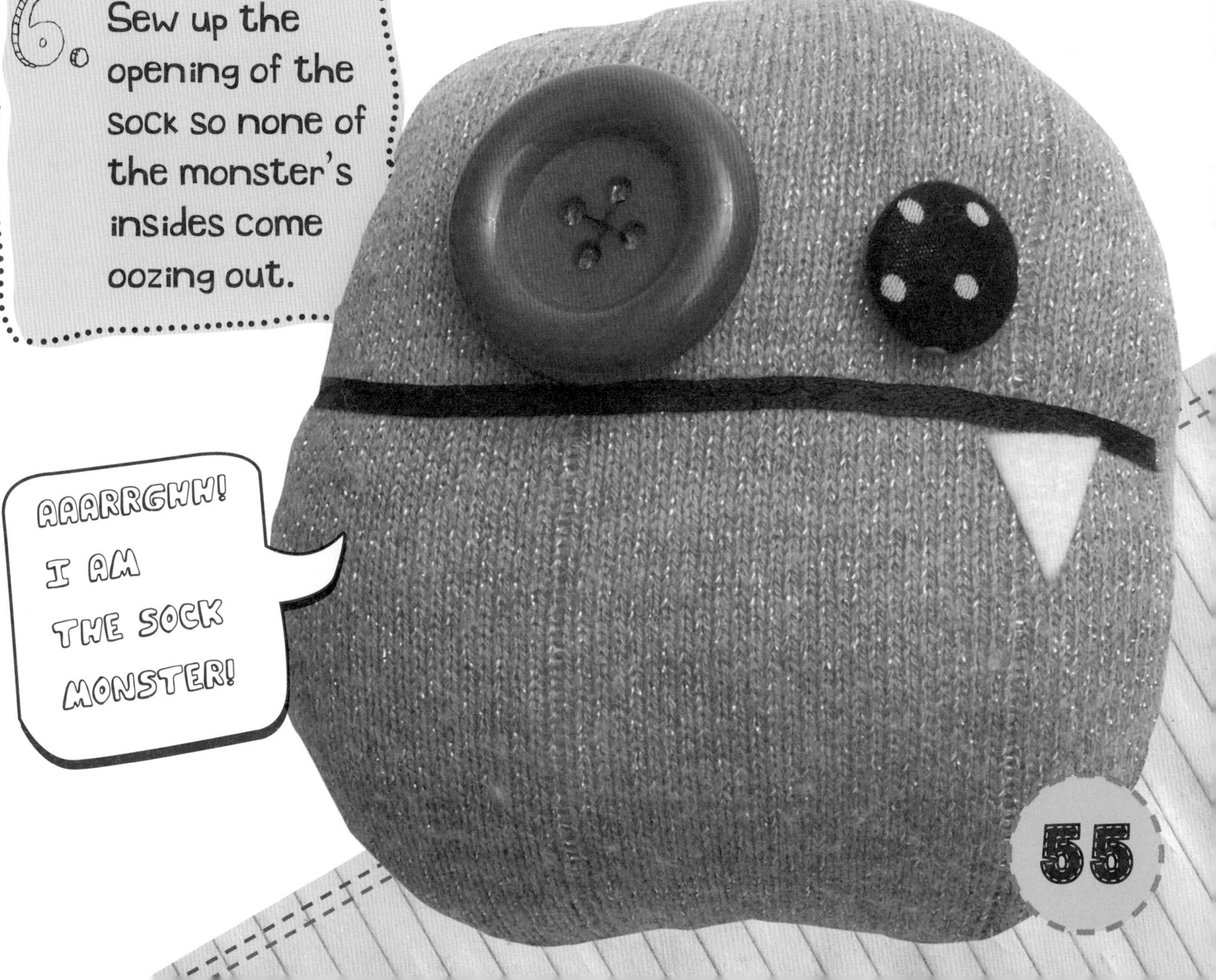

AAARRGHH! I AM THE SOCK MONSTER!

GLUE

55

SOCK RABBIT

Move up to the next level in sock projects by making this sock rabbit. It combines a sock with felt for an even more professional look.

To make this super-cute rabbit, YOU'LL NEED:

- ◉ 1 sock
- ◉ 2 buttons
- ◉ Black sewing thread
- ◉ 1 circle of felt, 2 inches across
- ◉ 2 pieces of fabric, cut to the shape of bunny ears
- ◉ Stuffing and white glue

HERE'S WHAT YOU DO:

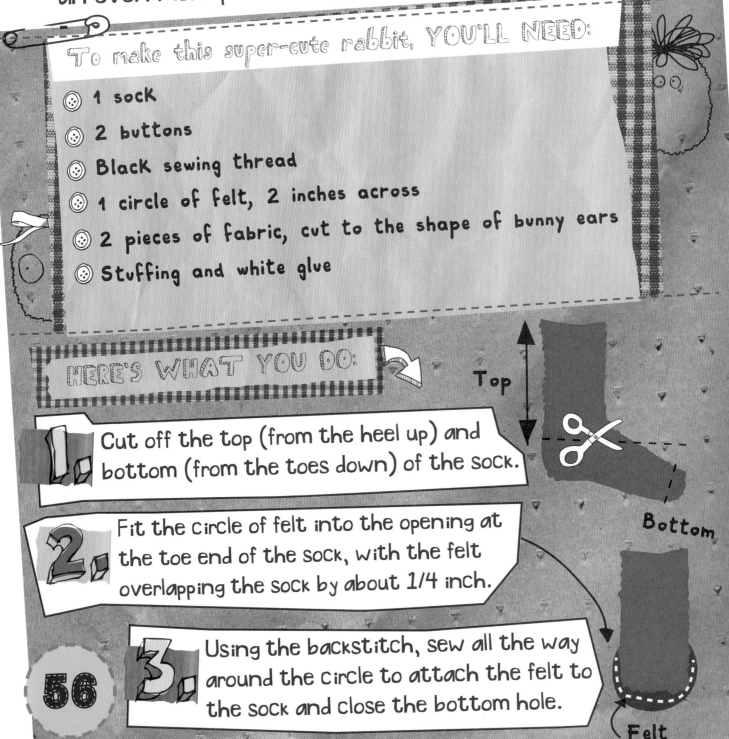

1. Cut off the top (from the heel up) and bottom (from the toes down) of the sock.

Top

Bottom

2. Fit the circle of felt into the opening at the toe end of the sock, with the felt overlapping the sock by about 1/4 inch.

3. Using the backstitch, sew all the way around the circle to attach the felt to the sock and close the bottom hole.

Felt

56

4. To give your bunny eyes, sew the buttons to the sock.

5. To give your bunny a nose, sew diagonally across several times.

6. Stuff your rabbit with cotton stuffing, beans, or even tissues.

7. Pin the ears in place at the top of the rabbit, placing the ends just slightly inside the opening at the top of the sock.

8. Sew across the opening, using the backstitch to close the hole and attach the ears all at once.

FABRIC FLOWER BROOCH

This little blossom adds a perfect touch to any outfit. Depending on the material you choose, it can be cutesy and girlie or edgy and cool ... whatever your style may be.

YOU'LL NEED:

- Patterned fabric cut into 7 petal shapes
- Felt cut into 7 petal shapes (same size as the patterned fabric)
- A pretty button or patch
- Colorful sewing thread
- A safety pin

HERE'S WHAT YOU DO:

1. Place the patterned fabric petal and the felt petal together with the pattern facing inward.

2. Sew around the petal, leaving a small gap.

3. Use the small gap to turn the petal the right way out.

4. Repeat steps 1 to 3 for the 6 other petals.

ALERT! Hard part!

5. For a cool folded effect, pinch the bottom of a petal and sew through it, and then do this for all the other petals, so you're threading through each of them and pinching them together as you go. Go around several times to make sure your flower is secure.

6. Sew a button to the middle of the flower.

7. Use a safety pin to attach the brooch to your clothes, scarf, bag, or hat, or glue a brooch pin back to the back to be super professional—especially if this is a gift!

Flower Power

SPARKLY ROCK CHICK BUTTON

If wooden dolls aren't your style, how about a sparkly rock chick button to totally rock your outfit?

YOU'LL NEED:

A pin button with a cool pattern
Sequins
6 ribbons, each 3 inches long
3 ribbons, each 4 inches long

TIP: Ribbons don't have to be actual ribbons. Try cutting straps from an old nightie or bag!

Sewing thread and white glue

HERE'S WHAT YOU DO:

1. Make each short piece of ribbon into a loop and glue the ends to the back of the button to make this pattern.

GLUE

2. Glue as many sequins as you like to the three longer ribbons. Wait for them to dry.

3. Sew the top of the three sequined ribbons together.

4. Glue the sequined ribbons to the back of the button.

TIP: Use a lot of glue and put something heavy on the ribbons so they dry securely in place.

5. Pin to your shirt, bag, or hat, and bring this fashion statement wherever you go!

SWEET DREAMS eye masks

Do you or someone you know need a good night's sleep? Try out this super-sweet eye mask for sweet dreams and peaceful nights.

YOU'LL NEED:

- ☆ 1 piece of patterned fabric, cut to the eye mask template
- ☆ 1 piece of soft fabric, also eye-mask shaped (this needs to be super-soft—an old fleece sweater works well)
- ☆ 1 piece of thick fabric, also eye-mask shaped, to be used as the middle padding
- ☆ 2 pieces of ribbon, each about 12 inches long
- ☆ Felt or buttons to decorate
- ☆ Sewing thread

HERE'S WHAT YOU DO:

1. First, decorate the patterned fabric. This Night-Night mask has words sewn on felt using a split running stitch, but you could try buttons or ribbon or other felt shapes to adorn the mask with loveliness, too.

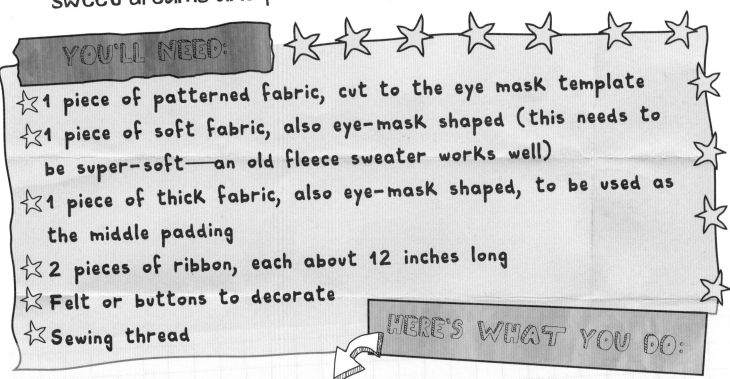

Try quirky patterns, too. How about a face on a face?

62